The Future

written and drawn by
JOHNNUS FARMANUS
(alias John Farman)
in the year of our Lord
Nineteen Hundred and Ninety-Nine

MACMILLAN
CHILDREN'S BOOKS

Titles in the **HISTORY in a HURRY** *series*

All **HISTORY in a HURRY** *titles can be ordered at your local bookshop or are available by post from Book Service by Post (tel: 01624 675137).*

First published 1999 by Macmillan Children's Books
a division of Macmillan Publishers Limited
25 Eccleston Place, London SW1W 9NF
Basingstoke and Oxford

Associated companies throughout the world

ISBN 0 330 37649 7

3 5 7 9 8 6 4 2

A CIP catalogue record for this book is available from the British Library.

Printed and bound in Great Britain by Mackays of Chatham plc, Kent

CONTENTS

OFF WE GO!

If you've had the great good fortune to have read some of my other books in this series, you will probably have realized (unless you're a bit daft*) that they only deal with things that happened in the past. Having studied millions of years of history and written more than a dozen books covering our exotic past, I thought it would be a bit of a laugh to have a go at the Future. Let's face it, for once in my life, what *I* think about a subject is pretty much as good as what anyone else thinks. The best bit is that my editor (she's the one called *Ed.* who writes all those nit-picking comments at the bottom of the pages) won't be able to have a go at me for lack of accuracy!

The Future's in the Past

The safest way of guessing what *is* going to happen in the future is to look a bit closer at what's gone on in the past. If, like me, you believe that one thing leads to another, you will realize that just about everything on this earth has developed from something else. When an early ape, for instance, worked out that hitting his mate with a lump of wood had far more effect than just using his bare hands, he was well on the way to inventing not only the first weapon, but also the first tool (and his first enemy?).

* Which they must be to have read any of your other books. Ed.

Counting on the Future

When the Egyptians thought up the bead abacus (for counting) in 500 BC, they little realized they had started a ball rolling (or should that be bead sliding) that would eventually lead to the mechanical calculator. In 1834 when Charles Babbage introduced his *Analytical Machine*, he had stumbled on the first principles of the computer. But it took until 1951 for the first commercial computer, the *Univac 1*, to go on sale in the States.

The computer, without any doubt, has been the greatest invention since the hula-hoop* and is the only tool which is capable of designing bigger and better versions of itself. It is used in practically everything we manufacture today. Scary as it may seem, computers are meddling in just about every aspect of our lives.

Iffy Internet

The world-wide Internet is a sort of communications mutant that doubles its size every year, and in the year 2000 there will be no less than 2,000 million computers yapping away to each

* I think you mean the wheel. Ed

other. This will have repercussions far outside just the stuff mentioned in this book. It will transform the very centre of our society and its culture.

It's the old people I feel sorry for. Let's face it, an oldie in his eighties today was born into a world of no radio, no television, no plane travel, and even no McDonald's. No wonder most of them roll their eyes at the mere mention of the Internet.

Revolution Ahoy!

Ever since the first man/monkey swung down from the trees and gave 'being civilized' his best shot, there have been three major stages in his development:*

☆ *The Agrarian Revolution*

The first was the Agrarian (agricultural) Revolution, when man realized that, with a little forethought, he wouldn't have to go hunting and gathering every single day to make sure of a ready supply of grub.

* A touch simple, don't you think? Ed

☆ *The Industrial Revolution*

Then, thousands of years later and only a couple of centuries ago (just *three* average lifetimes), man discovered that he could actually make machines do his dirty work for him. Even now, as we lurch into the next millennium, the effects of this Industrial Revolution continue to create a huge split in the world between those societies that have been through it (like us), and those poor beggars who are still waiting for it to happen. Many believe that *all* the problems in the world today are caused by the conflicts between those that *are* industrialized and those that ain't. In other words – the Haves and the Have Nots.

☆ *The Revolution with No Name*

But while the majority of the world is waiting to be brought even slightly up to date, the rest of us – America, Europe, Japan, etc. – have left the Industrial Revolution well behind and are diving headlong into a new one, a thousand times mightier and a million trillion *zillion* times more exciting than anything that has gone before. As yet, this revolution hasn't got a name – as names are usually given to things after they've happened* – but just because it's got no name doesn't mean that it's not very, very real.

The Future

You will notice that in this book, at the beginning of each chapter, I will tend to talk about what we already know about

* How about the Technological Revolution? Ed

a particular subject. This is then followed by advances that are already being planned. At the end of each chapter, in the part called *Farman's Fantasy Future*, I go a bit mad – describing how I personally reckon that the future might go. If it actually happens, please don't blame me. If it doesn't, please don't blame me either.

Chapter 1

THE END OF THE WORLD?

Before we get into the future, let's see if we've even got one. Some would say that if you've got anything big planned, you should probably drop everything right now and get on with it. They're the ones that believe the predictions of head prophet *Nostradamus*. This clever old Frenchman reckoned that the events leading to Armageddon (or the End of the World) were due to start in – wait for it – 1999, with a horrendous 27-year World War. This is a trifle worrying, as Nostradamus also seems to have predicted (rather successfully):

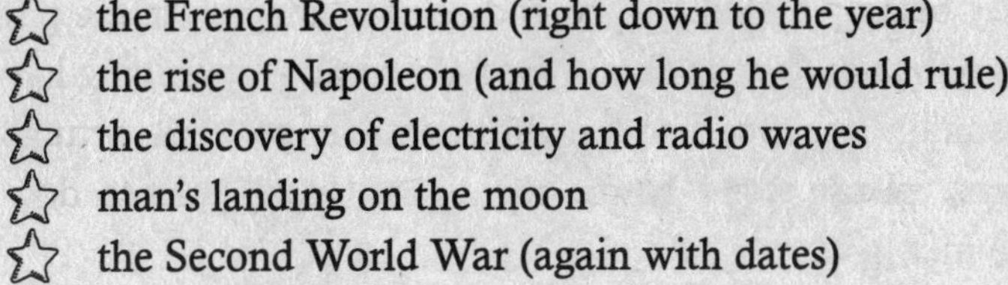

- the French Revolution (right down to the year)
- the rise of Napoleon (and how long he would rule)
- the discovery of electricity and radio waves
- man's landing on the moon
- the Second World War (again with dates)
- the time and manner of his own death . . .

. . . and a whole load of other stuff – all this back in . . . 1557!

Don't Panic!

But before you get too worked up about all this End-of-the-World talk and start being nice to your brothers and sisters and confessing to all the bad things you've done in your life (like putting the goldfish in the freezer – don't!), it might be just worth considering that Christians have already predicted the

End of the World in AD 996, 1186, 1553, 1665, 1866, 1931, 1945, 1954, 1960, 1965, 1967 and 1994. The Moslems, on the other hand, were convinced that life would end on the day the first man walked on the moon (which would have been 1969). I don't know about you, but looking around, I think they should all be feeling a bit silly.

Useless Fact No. 1050

In 4500 BC the Great Flood, as described in the Bible, was supposed to have ended the world by killing everyone off. God, who was a trifle miffed with the human race, made it rain for 40 days and 40 nights, drowning everything apart from this rather creepy old geezer called Noah, his family, and two of every kind of animal. Presumably God never had anything against fish – since a flood wasn't exactly gonna drown them.

Anyway, old Nostradamus wasn't *all* doom and gloom. He also predicted that after this frightful War To End All Wars (from 1999 to 2026) there'd be a thousand years of peace – but it wouldn't be much use to us lot (as we'd probably be dead).

Mind you, after that particular thousand years things wouldn't be that much fun as, according to him, in the year 3755 a load of asteroids will hit the earth, covering the surface with fire. Then, 40-odd years after that, the game will be up completely, when the poor old earth will be totally consumed by the sun. So don't plan anything in about 1,800 years' time that you can't get out of.

On the Other Hand

If none of the End of the World dates mentioned so far grab you, you could always try one of the following (or just make up your own).

Old Buddha (head of the Buddhists) reckoned that it will all go pear-shaped in the year 2000 (close or what?) . . . while the Egyptians thought that the world would end in a massive ball of fire in 2001. But don't celebrate *too* much at the end of 2001 – you're not necessarily in the clear yet: the Mayan Indians of Ancient Mexico predicted that Time's-Up will be in 2012. I suppose that's a bit better.

The End is Nigh?

There are many ways of writing this little book. We could believe that . . .

1. Nostradamus and Co. were right.
2. We'll be smashed to pieces by a stray asteroid or something.
3. We'll eventually pollute ourselves to death.
4. One day little green men will come from a far-off planet, hover over Enfield Station, and then zap us to bits.

But, unfortunately, any of these 'futures' would result in a book that would look rather like this . . .

. . . or you *could* believe (like I do) that the human race, despite all its awfulness, will always manage to stop short of totally destroying itself. One thing you'll notice about *my* future is that, unlike most others, it's quite jolly. If, by any chance, the world does pull itself apart in a couple of years' time, and if you think you'll want your money back – tough! I won't be around to *give* it, and – even better – you won't be around to *get* it . . . and anyway there wouldn't be anything to spend it on. So there!

So here we go, let's put on our happy hats and Carry On Predicting.

Chapter 2

FOOD FOR ALL? EATING OUR WAY INTO THE FUTURE

With a population that rises every time you blink, sooner or later there won't be enough grub to go round. 'Hold on,' I hear you cry, 'we've reached that point already, haven't we?' Why else, night after night, in our cosy homes, just after we've scoffed our deep-pan pizzas and oven-ready chips, do we have to endure tragic pictures of hopelessly thin Third-World children on our tellies?

Well, we jolly well shouldn't have to. Quite simply, at the moment, there *is* enough food for everyone, and don't let

anyone tell you otherwise. Just think of all those mountains of corn, butter and heaven-knows-what-else, sitting in massive Eurobarns (or whatever they're called) doing absolutely nothing. The problem lies in a single word – well, two single words – politics and greed.* The reason that this food doesn't get to the mouths of the poor folk who crave it most is because so many of the greedy, useless, self-seeking, inefficient, lazy good-for-nothings (have I left anything out?), who we seem to have elected to run our world, spend most of their time bickering about, or even profiting from, their misery. Whose job is it to distribute it? How much should it be sold for? Who should pay for it? Who deserves it most? Is there any cash to be made from the deal?

Larders in Space

But what's all this got to do with the future? Well, in my version of how it will all pan out, no one will go hungry because of distribution mess-ups. Within our lifetimes, there will, with a bit of luck, be a World Government – and part of its duties will be to run a Global Food Bureau. Every year, each country will promise a percentage of the food it produces. This will be stored in massive cosmic warehouses orbiting the world. Food could then be sent quickly to any place where people, for whatever reason, are running short in the old grub department. I think I'd like to order a curry now, please!

Kid Alert!

Even so, *if* earth folk keep on doing what they like doing most – reproducing themselves (to put it politely) – there will

* That's *three* single words actually. Ed

inevitably come a point at which the earth simply cannot grow enough to feed everyone. Well, certainly not by using the farming methods that we use at the moment. In the 1980s, the World Health Organization predicted that, when the five-billionth child was born, it would then be beyond the possibility of the earth to feed him or her (let alone his 4,999,999,999 brothers and sisters) . . . Slight problem. We're well past that figure now. In fact, there's now six billion, and still going. They were wrong – but they won't always be wrong – what's to be done when we reach a proper food crisis? (The United Nations reckon that by the year 2050 there'll be nine billion people on the planet!)

Useless Fact No. 1053

With three children born every second, by the time you finish this chapter (if you're a fast reader) there will be roughly 1,250 more little perishers arriving for supper.

The Perfect Pill?

Some of those who write science fiction or predictions of the future, reckon that in the next 50 years or so some boffin will come up with a nice little tablet that will satisfy all our needs nutrition-wise – but I don't think so. It seems that each year we become more and more obsessed by food; either in the third world (because there isn't enough) or over here where we seem to have too much (especially if those ghastly, never-ending foodie programs on telly are anything to go by). But if we don't start eating nutrition pills, how will the farmers keep up with the demand for more and more food?

Water, Water Everywhere

The answer to the problem is slopping about all around us, but so far we have failed to see it. People who know these things tell us that 80% of the earth is covered by sea and, according to some, this water is getting deeper and therefore bigger, because of global warming (which has a habit of melting the polar icecaps). Up till now farmers have struggled to grow food in spite of terrible weather, disease or pollution – but only on the dry bits of the world. Both crops *and* livestock are prone to the whims of Mother Nature – and the grumpy old bag can be a cruel mistress.

But conditions under the sea are always pretty much the same and practically anything can grow in it* (as long as we don't clog it up with rubbish). The sea could, therefore, be 'farmed' just like the land, and many experts predict that's exactly what will happen, and not too far from now.

But what I want to know is, how can you farm underwater without getting your tractor wet?

Home Under the Range

Has it ever struck you that the only animals that have been threatened by extinction are those that have been hunted. I mean, we never worry about cows, chickens, pigs or sheep running out, because they are bred and cared for by us – for us. Not because we particularly like 'em, but because we like eating 'em and wearing their skins.**

Whaleboys Ahoy!

For centuries now, the amazingly big blue whale – up to 150 tons of valuable meat and oil, and worth a cool £15,000-plus on the open market – has been chased and hunted into near extinction. They still are, by (some would say) stupid, blinkered nations like the Norwegians, the Russians and the Japanese. However, why not rear whales just like cattle or, even better, like trout (on account of the fact that whales need water)? Great idea! But why wouldn't they just swim away?

Cos they wouldn't. Read on . . .

* Lambs? Ed

** Chicken skins? Ed

Whale Farms

Arthur C. Clarke, probably the greatest sci-fi writer and crystal-ball gazer ever, predicted that, in the not-too-distant future, vast (thousands of miles across) whale ranches will exist in the middle of our oceans, patrolled by gangs of whaleboys in speedboats and miniature subs. These massive creatures could be fenced in by sonar pulses, which not only the whales would refuse to cross, but also their main enemy (apart from us) – the killer whale. By the way, Mr Clarke also said that whale milk is richer than any other milk and could be processed to taste just like cows.*

If you're worried about the poor whales – well, yes, I admit

* Don't you mean cows' *milk*? Ed

they'd end up the same way (dead) but you can bet that they'd meet their end in a more humane way than they do now.

And it's not just whales that could be farmed like this, but also tuna, shark, cod, seals, turtles, mermaids and all the other sorts of creatures that we still hunt for in such a haphazard, cruel and, let's face it, downright silly manner.

Useless Fact No. 1058

If you ever have calamari, those little rings of squid that look (and sometimes taste) like rubber bands cooked in batter, just consider that their big brother squids can grow up to two tons in weight. OK, they don't look that pretty, but that's one heck of a meal. They too could be farmed relatively easily . . .

Funny Food Alert

As I write, there's a terrible fuss going on in the papers about genetic engineering (or, as they tactfully label it, 'genetic modification') of the food we eat. I looked 'genetic engineering' up in the dictionary and this is what it said: 'The directed alteration of genetic material by intervention in genetic processes.' In other words, mucking around splicing bits of genes with other bits of genes.

But the fuss, so far, hasn't been about the taste, texture or any of the other qualities of the food in question. It's all been about our fears of monkeying around with things that we and even the scientists don't know too much about. Maybe they've got a point. I mean, I don't want to grow another head just because I've eaten half a tin of genetically modified baked beans, thank you very much; any more than I'd have wanted to be that poor mouse, who was in the papers recently, with a massive human ear sticking out of its back (even if he did have the best hearing in Mouse City).*

* I don't think that had anything to do with GM food. Ed

Anyone for Whaleburgers?

The point is that genetic modification of food, or anything else, is still in its infancy and we defenceless citizens are a trifle worried because our government can't convince us that the products, or should I say, the results of eating the products, have been tested thoroughly enough. But it's only a matter of time . . . and ethics (the actual rights and wrongs of it). Whether it's right to breed a whale that tastes of beef (or a cow that can swim underwater and grow to 100 tons) is not for me

to say, but if it means that we won't have to watch helplessly from the comfort of our armchairs as those poor little mites in the Third World starve to death, I suppose I can go along with it. Crikey, let's look on the bright side for once. We could have all sorts of weird and wonderful foods on our supermarket shelves, like . . .

☆ Potatoes genetically crossed with prawns for instant prawn cocktail crisps.

☆ Huge hens with four legs and no beaks that pluck themselves.*

☆ A cross between the haricot bean and the tomato, for ready-made baked beans.

Any other suggestions? Stick 'em on a postcard and send them to my publishers.

Interplanetary Farming

Despite everything I've said about maximizing food production on Earth (and under the sea), the human race will eventually have to face the fact that there are just too many mouths to feed off the land and sea available to farm. Within the next 30 years there's a fair chance we'll not only be inhabiting, but producing food on the nearer planets or even on orbiting cosmofarms. 'But how can that be done?' I hear you cry again. You can't, for instance, just go up to the moon, scatter a few seeds and hope for the best – everyone knows that. However, the discovery of 6.6 billion tons of ice on the moon has certainly made it more imaginable (and helped to make the moon the most valuable piece of real estate in our local solar system).

Ice means water, which could mean agriculture and industry (and something to drink). Not only that, but water, when broken down into hydrogen and oxygen, forms the basic ingredients of . . . rocket fuel. Useful, eh! (In order to see how we might go about it, see Chapter 7.)

* How? Ed

 **Farman's Fantasy Future** 

2013

Following a recent TV Wildlife Special on giant squid, introduced by Sir David Attenborough (now 87), Atlantic Whale Farms Inc. decide to introduce them into their water-ranches. The price of calamari is expected to drop substantially when these monsters are farmed intensively.

2016

The genetic modification of seaweed has meant that practically all land-based vegetable crops can now be cloned and grown in vast quantities in the oceans of the world. The latest Honda Sub-tractor will reap and process the new crops – and deliver them to superports throughout the world.

2019

Lulu, a French poodle which is the result of research into the possible genetic adaptation of carnivores (in the hope that they

can digest and thrive on grass like cows), becomes the first dog to happily trim the lawn while requiring no other food. Similar experiments on humans will follow shortly. The only problem so far is the aggressive mooing sound that Lulu makes when the postman approaches . . .

2021

The discovery that all the infertile soil on earth, even deserts, can be enriched by drawing nitrogen from the atmosphere causes mass panic amongst the farming community. Massive food surpluses are predicted and millions of farmers throughout the world will be forced to look for alternative employment.

2025

It is revealed at the headquarters of Intergrub Inc. (the giant conglomerate made up from the world's six largest food producers) that most of the world's food could soon be grown under glass domes with their own eco-atmosphere on Mars – or any of the new planets visited in the last couple of years. It will be brought back to earth by massive cosmotankers.

Chapter 3

MOVING AROUND IN THE FUTURE

There are still people who live in country areas who have never travelled much further than the edge of their own town or village. Only a hundred or so years ago, it took the best part of a day to go from London to, say, Brighton by horse and carriage. To cross the Channel, one would have had to wait for the wind and the rest of the weather to be just right before setting sail and even then it could take ages.

If, a century ago, you'd suggested to your fellow stagecoach passenger that in only a hundred years (just one and a half average lifetimes) you'd be able to drive to Paris under the sea and reach Australia in a few hours in a plane that goes faster than sound, he'd have probably jumped out to search for a straitjacket.

Any graph, like the one on the next page, mapping the advances in technology through history, shows that the line going up has never been steeper than now. This is due entirely to the computer, which increasingly spends more of its time simply improving itself. To guess with any accuracy what might happen to transport in the near, middle and distant future is pretty much impossible. Therefore, what I am about to suggest may seem pretty far-fetched, but it is based on the predictions of eminent scientists and future-gazers. Here we go.

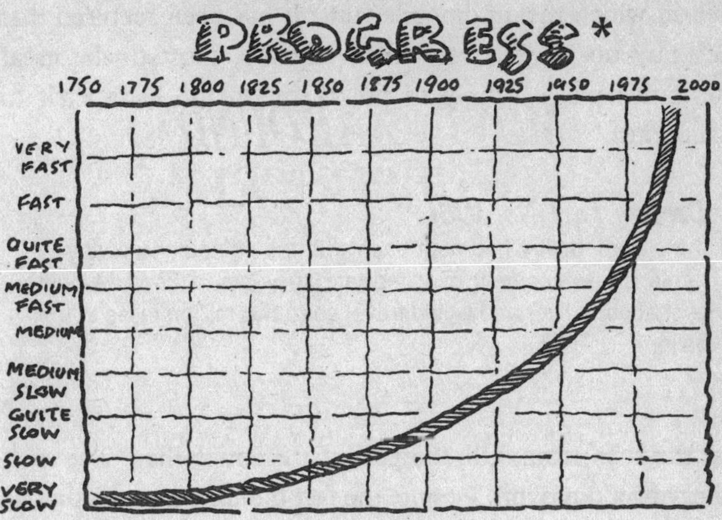

Short Term

The car we drive today, despite all its seemingly hi-tech gizmos, is about as modern as a carrot (before genetic modification, of course). The internal combustion engine that still powers your car is not an awful lot different in principle to the one invented by Nikolaus August Otto in 1876. Even the very latest, most snazzy models are only variations on a well-worn theme. This old-fashioned petrol- or diesel-driven engine is expensive to run, uses resources that could be used much better elsewhere and is a major polluter of our atmosphere. It's obvious, therefore, that someone's got to do something about it – and pretty soon. But why haven't they?

One of the main reasons that nothing's been done is that practically no big money is ever spent on research. Why? Because the exceedingly rich oil companies are forever worried about the prospect that one day someone might replace the

* Very scientific. Ed

fuel on which the automobile runs. It has been reported that they buy up, at relatively small expense, most of the great alternative ideas, simply to put them on the back shelf to gather dust.

Useless Fact No. 1061

If the car industry had kept pace with the computer industry in terms of development over the last 30 years, a Ferrari would cost about a fiver and would travel up to two million miles to the gallon!

But the rush is on. Oil companies are now falling over each other to get out of oil. Despite the fact that there is a surplus at the moment, it's well-known that nobody is pumping it back *into* the Earth, so it has to run out some day.

Fully Charged

There are several alternatives to petrol, but none so far have got past the experimental stage. Most hopeful of all, in the very short term, is the petrol/battery-driven car. This uses a tiny petrol-driven motor which runs in short bursts simply to keep a big battery (from which the car is powered) charged up. This vehicle, so the inventors reckon, could travel for hundreds of miles on one gallon of petrol, and would give off practically no noxious gases.

Here Comes The Sun

But that's just a half measure. The real answer lies, and always has, in the use of things that aren't going to run out. Electricity generated by the massive rise and fall of the sea is now successfully used in the USA, France, Japan and Russia. But the real biggy has to be the conversion of sunlight into energy. Experimental solar-powered vehicles have been around for donkey's years, but have only been a moderate success, mainly because of the size of the 'collecting' surface necessary to generate the power to push something heavy along. But it seems odd that, despite the fact that all our spacecraft use solar power when in orbit and millions of houses rely on it for heat and light, it is beyond the wit of man to solve this problem. I reckon, however, that within the next 30 years your mum or dad's petrol-powered car will be gathering dust in a museum and we'll all be whizzing around in totally silent, practically-free-to-run, sun-powered motors.

Wot! No Driver

The trouble with having soft, squishy things (us) travelling in hard, sharp things (cars) is that when one hard, sharp thing hits another hard, sharp thing, the soft, squishy things inside get – er – squished. Human beings are vulnerable and also capable of making mistakes. Computers aren't. Therefore it stands to reason that letting people drive, make mistakes and possibly kill themselves or others is a trifle daft. If computers were driving the cars, the world would be a much safer place. After all, you would never get a self-respecting computer trying to steer while dialling a number on its mobile phone, drinking a cup of coffee, tuning the radio, getting the map off the back seat *and* keeping the kids amused.

Also, computers wouldn't need road signs to tell them where to go – they'd already know. In the next 40 years or so, probably in America (where most good things get thought of first*), it will be possible to get in your car, tell it where to go (personal voice recognition is already standard on many PCs) and sit back to have a drink (even an alcoholic one!). Through sensors on every highway, cars will plot their own course using a grid lodged in their computer hard-drives (with a built in sensor to avoid traffic jams).

* Like nuclear weapons? Ed

Useless Fact No. 1063

If this all seems far-fetched – get this. As I write, all new RAC members now receive a little gadget, as a free gift, that you put on your windscreen to tell you about delays on the roads ahead. It operates through sensors installed by Cellnet along all the motorways, which log the speed of passing traffic and relay it back to the individual driver. They really do work (I've got one).

Off to School

Fully automatic cars will mean that children will be able to do the school run on their own and old codgers won't have to give up their cars when they become too gaga to drive. They'll simply tell their car to pick them up at a certain time or just phone it on their own personal phone (everyone, including children, will probably have wristwatch phones within five years). Also, with personal voice recognition instead of an ignition key, car theft will become merely a rather quaint memory. Almost best of all, drinking and driving might become legal if the computer takes over all the hard work.*

Space Once Again

It's weird. There were men walking about on the moon from 1969 to 1972 and since then . . . absolutely nothing. The reason? At $500 million a pop, it cost far too much to get there, and governments can't afford to do it any more. To get to Mars, the most obvious planet for attempts at early colonization, it was estimated that it would cost a ludicrous $400 billion and that frightened off the American government big time.

But, if you read Adrian Berry's fantastic book *The Next 500 Years,* you'll soon realize that it won't be governments that

* Trust you to think of that, Mr Farman. Ed

eventually conquer space. It will be the massive international corporations like Microsoft, Ford, Sony, Coca-Cola or even dear old Richard Branson's Virgin – who will do it for the one and only totally trustworthy motive – profit!

But, apart from the ever-growing satellite communications industry, the major players have so far kept away from the wide blue yonder. One of the reasons is that it's all very well sending the rockets *up*, but there has to be a way of getting the darn things back down in one piece, otherwise costs go through the clouds. I mean, imagine if you ran an airline like they do the space industry – dropping the engines in the sea every time they'd got the plane into the air – expensive or what!

Privatization

The good news is that private companies have already started work on space launchers and the American aeronautics company McDonnell Douglas are well into the development of a one-stage rocket ship that can be launched by just a couple of people and that won't have to end up in the cosmic breaker's yard each time it goes for a jaunt. Better still, they reckon they know of a fuel that won't pollute the atmosphere and won't blow up every five minutes. In *The Next*

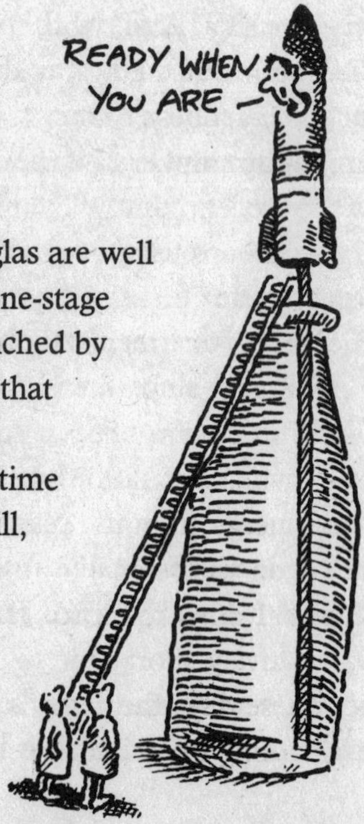

500 Years, Mr Berry reckons that in 20 years from now it will cost no more to go to the moon than to, say, Australia, and that all of us will have the chance to fly in space before we're very much older.

Faster and Further

Unfortunately, all this is kids' stuff, compared to the sort of craft that will be necessary to travel any great distance space-wise, in a timespan worth bothering about. Adrian Berry suggests a few ways of reaching these speeds: small nuclear explosions set off behind the spacecraft, which literally shove it along, or maybe antimatter engines in which particles of matter and antimatter collide to make the biggest explosions ever (a hundred times more powerful than nuclear bangs), which could push a 12,000-ton monster along at jolly nearly 100 million kph. But the best and most possible of all is the *Interstellar Ramjet* (doesn't that sound groovy?), which would suck, from the atmosphere it's travelling through, atoms of the very gas, hydrogen, that would power its nuclear fusion engines (with scoops using huge magnetic fields thousands of kilometres across). The faster it would go, therefore, the faster it would be *able* to go – up to 750 million kph.

Other scientists think all this talk of rocket ships dull and old-fashioned, preferring the idea of massive Solar Wings (see Chapter 7) which could achieve incredible speeds using nothing but energy from the sun. At those sorts of speeds, a trip to the moon will seem like a stroll to the corner shop.

Ridiculous? I don't think so. Just to show how things can change, a relatively short time ago only scientists visited the Antarctic. These days the place is flooded with tourists each summer. Anything's possible – see!

Useless Fact No. 1066

Oddly enough, the greatest worry about travelling at high speeds in space would be the possibility of being hit by space debris that could smash the craft to pieces. Some believe the answer to this would be to shape the ship a bit like a paper dart – which is exactly what all those early sci-fi writers thought!

Farman's Fantasy Future

2005

Revolution in air travel. Instead of hanging around in crowded air terminals, enduring hours in cramped planes, eating dodgy food and watching soppy movies, passengers can now take the option of travelling as *freight*! For a fraction of the fare they can be anaesthetized at a local travel centre, transported to the airport and, while sleeping in a padded, air-conditioned casket, loaded onto a plane, whisked off to their destination and woken with a complimentary drink at the other end.

2008

Electric cars now take 50% of the market. They can travel 650 km per recharge.

2009

Volkswagen announce the first car made out of carbon-reinforced rubber with an internal floating passenger capsule. Tests have shown that even at impacts of 160 kph the car simply bounces back to its original shape and the passengers (provided they are strapped in) remain a bit shaken but unhurt.

2010

The last subsonic plane, the dear old Boeing 950, goes out of service today. All earthly aircraft are now supersonic.

2014

From 1 August all cars are required to go on automatic drive on motorways. The *Honda 475 Robosteer* can now be fitted to the onboard computer of most makes of car manufactured in the last three years.

2016

Motor racing as a sport ends as the Maclaren Formula One racing team confess that the driver of the car that won the Belgian Grand Prix this year took no part in the operation.

2020

Sales of the *Ford Gyrostar*, a compact, family, solar-assisted helicopter, now officially outnumber those of Ford's land-limited vehicles in America. With onboard computer navigation, controlled by fully automated state flight control (no human error possible), there have been no fatal gyro accidents in five years.

2027

The latest phone-wristwatch by Seiko features a button that when pressed can locate your position anywhere in the world to within a two-metre square. Essential equipment for adventurous travellers and dodgy taxi drivers.

2033

The largest traffic pile-up ever recorded occurs just south of Los Angeles on the 28-lane Interstate Freeway and involves 720 cars. An electrical storm caused all the in-car computers to fail. Thanks to carbon/rubber bodywork, no serious damage to vehicles is reported and nobody suffers more than a severe bouncing.

2037

Virgin Airways, the last all-British airline, announce their first daily flights to Moonbase 1, the only holiday resort where you can sip a cocktail by the light of the silvery Earth.

2057

Owing to the horrendous eco-damage from America's ever-increasing road grid, an ambitious plan was started 20 years ago to put all human transportation underground. It is now completed, ahead of schedule, due to the gigantic trillion dollar *Branson Tunneldiver,* which can cut through the earth at the rate of 30 km per day. The new, pneumatic underground system can carry people at 750 kph in great comfort and at relatively small cost.

2058

Britain announce that pollution levels are one twentieth of what they were in the year 2000. This is largely due to all non-local road transport being safely underground and the recycling of all industrial by-products before reaching the atmosphere.

4050

Experimenters at AFR (Atomic Fragmentation and Re-assembly) announce that the method is now completely safe and tested. People wishing to travel anywhere in the galaxy (even Ruislip) will soon be able to be dematerialized in their local travel port, entered into the *Microsoft Travelnet 7 System* and re-constituted at the port of their choice. London to Sydney is expected to take three seconds. New York, of course, will be shorter.

Chapter 4

FEELING BETTER IN THE FUTURE

Despite all the fuss we make about our polluted environment, genetically modified soya, mad cows, perforated ozone layers, nuclear fallout, crowded air-lanes or Celine Dion, we humans are living longer than ever. Life expectancy, as we leap into the next millennium, is on the up and up.

Look at history again. If you'd lived in Roman times, two millennia ago, you'd have been lucky to reach your 28th birthday (especially if you were a Christian). Even in the middle of the last century, the average age for men to pop their clogs in this country was no more than 50. (Women generally live a bit longer.) Today we can all expect to keep going until well into our seventies (provided we continue to look both ways when crossing the road).

National Health

Why is this happening? Well, despite what all those alternative medicine people – the herbalists, aromatherapists, spiritual healers, hydropaths, endogenous endocrinotherapists or acupuncturists, homeopaths, naturopaths, psychopaths* – would have us believe, our conventional health system (the one that everyone moans about) is keeping us out of the ground progressively longer – and it'll keep on getting better.

Thanks to new drug treatments, coupled with the study of

* What??? Ed

trendy subjects like genetics, laser surgery (see below), micro-surgery (very small), nano-surgery (very, very small) and much, much better after-care treatment – anyone who is now, say, 12 or below can reasonably hope to live to 100 years old. Eventually, due to the newly discovered superoxide enzymes which can be made to protect our DNA, your children (or maybe your children's children) should end up having to blow out over 140 candles on their birthday cakes.

Useless Fact No. 1069

In 1917 the king only had to send 110 telegrams of congratulation to those reaching 100 years old. Our poor queen now has to send over 3,000 (and that's an awful lot of stamp licking).

Useless Fact No. 1073

Just in case you needed to know, a laser is a device that utilizes the natural oscillations of atoms or molecules between energy levels for generating coherent electromagnetic radiation used in ultraviolet, visible or infrared regions of the spectrum. Now close your eyes and say that back to me.

Hands On

Recently, a chap who'd had his hand mangled in an accident had another one sewn on. Now, this is not quite as easy as it might sound. I expect you lot think it's just a question of nicking the hand off some recently deceased individual, making sure it's the right size and sex,* checking that it's the right hand (or the left) and the right way up and then simply getting out the old needle and thread. But, if you've ever seen one of those outside telephone junction boxes with millions of different-coloured wires all going different ways and all doing different things, you might get some idea of what's involved.

Every nerve, artery and muscle fibre must be perfectly matched and joined up (as well as matching the suntan). This, at present, can only be done by the most painstaking micro-surgery, carried out with a microscope linked to a TV monitor. Nano-surgery, a million times more magnified, is still just a twinkle in the surgeon's eye but, when perfected, it will mean

* Does sex make any difference? Ed

that the reconnection of all the various bits and pieces that we've carelessly injured or mislaid, will be a relatively simple affair (especially if you're good at those plastic assembly kits).

Deep Freeze for All

Cryogenics is the posh word for any work carried out using freezing to change the properties of what you're working on. It began in 1877 when oxygen was cooled down so much that it became liquid. By 1960 scientists could achieve temperatures of just a millionth of a degree above absolute zero (–273°C) . . . and that's pretty darn cold. Cryosurgery is the use of freezing techniques while working on diseased or dead human or animal tissue, and has been found to be successful on tonsils, haemorrhoids (piles – ouch!), warts, cataracts, cancerous tumours and, of course, frozen chickens. There have recently been successful treatments of the dreaded Parkinson's Disease (which causes involuntary movements and shaking), by freezing the part of the brain that goes wonky.

Auto-defrost

For years now, scientists have talked about the possibilities of freezing a living organism and bringing it back to life on demand. The main use of this would be for those suffering from illnesses from which, at present, there's no cure. Up till now, because scientists haven't perfected a way of reversing the process (i.e. thawing the patient out), there's a massive ethical problem. Many people, especially those in great pain, are willing to be deep-frozen, on the basis that one day there *will* be a way of not only bringing them back to life but making them better. The trouble is, the authorities who tell us what and what not to do won't allow the deep-freezing of an

otherwise alive person, because at present any assistance in this could be regarded as conspiracy to murder. It does, however, seem to be just a matter of time before a foolproof method of freezing and defrosting living tissue is found. Then, without any doubt, all hell will break loose, and it won't only be just amongst the sick. Mega-rich people will demand to be frozen until a cure for getting older is found. It will probably become the ultimate status symbol.

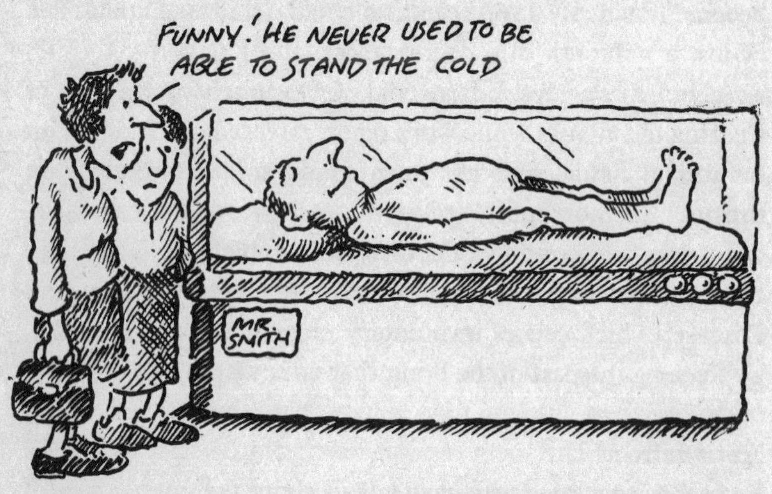

Farman's Fantasy Future

2003

Minnie, a mouse who has been frozen solid for six months, starts running about her cage again without so much as a shiver, having been successfully defrosted by scientists at Glasgow University. There is now no reason whatsoever why the computerized resuscitation programme shouldn't work for larger animals like us and doctors firmly believe it will take only a few years to perfect it.

2005

The World Court decide that assisting in suicides is to be made legal. The main result of this will be to open the door for Cryogenic Suspension (freezing). Up till now the first potential human guinea pigs were considered to be committing suicide, and those who did the freezing were seen as conspirators. His Holiness Pope Cliff I is said to be furious as, according to the Roman Catholic Church, life and death can only be determined by God. Anyway, he asks, what happens to the human soul while the body is frozen? Does it just hang around in a sort of heavenly waiting room until the body rejoins it, or does it start to look for someone else to hang out in?

2006

The worldwide cut-price funeral chain Dead Good Deals opens the first human freezer centre at their Los Angeles headquarters. This new building, capable of storing 10,000 bodies, is the first of hundreds planned throughout the world. Many thousands are queuing up to start the complicated legal process leading to freezing, including all four members of the Rolling Stones (who many believe are well past it anyway). Costs for freezing are steep – $30,000 for the initial 'big chill' and a further $10,000 a year for cold storage. Customers are expected to deposit enough money to cover themselves for 10 years at least, after which relatives will be approached and asked whether they want their nearest and dearest defrosted, or whether they are prepared to keep on paying the fridge rental and electricity bill.

2010

Smoking is now illegal in the United States. Falling demand and the imminent bankruptcy of tobacco manufacturers (due to the millions of lawsuits filed against them) has resulted in hardly any objections. The UK is expected to follow within two years. Hardened smokers are searching the galaxy for a planet (preferably ashtray-shaped) of their own.

2016

Keith Richards (of the Rolling Stones), 91, becomes the very first person to be defrosted successfully. Mr Richards, a previously heavy smoker, was not amused on coming round and asking for a cigarette, to find that, while frozen, they'd become illegal.

2024

Back in the year 2000 the average person was one third overweight due to lack of exercise and gross overeating. Now 85% of all westerners live within a couple of kilograms of their ideal bodyweight – owing to Weight Watcher International's patent monitoring system. This strap-on computerized device advises the wearer on his personal food and fitness needs. The device gives a mild electric shock if the wearer over-indulges. The *Slim-o-Shock* will be free to all on the World Welfare System within two years.

2051

At last prospective mothers can choose whether they want to go through all the bother of having a baby themselves. Womb-World UK, a branch of the Norwegian chain of childbirth centres, now offer a simulated birthing service to all couples. For £10,000 plus birth tax (15%) an embryo can be fertilized and nurtured in a revolutionary artificial womb until ready for a simulated birth (to the sound of soothing choral music) in the presence of both Mummy and Daddy. Inherent character faults (idleness, grumpiness, baldness, etc.) can be erased before birth (for a small extra charge) by the removal of any offending DNA at embryo stage.

Stop Press. Demonstrations are held in London by angry maternity clothing manufacturers, who claim they will soon be out of business.

2057

Internal organs can now be cloned by matching samples of DNA. People with thyroid, liver or pancreas problems can receive a 30-year guarantee with any new parts. Heavy drinkers need not apply.

2075

Scientists developing production-line robots in the automobile industry astound the world with the *Robosurge 3000*, the first

computer-programmed robot capable of carrying out complicated surgery on humans.

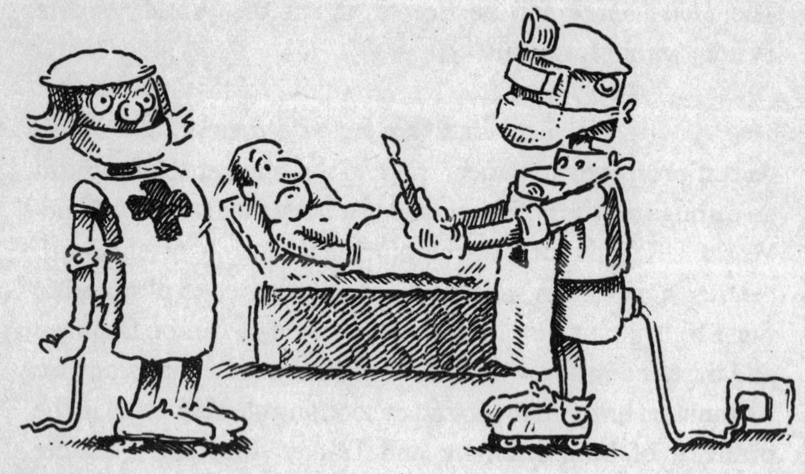

2081

Thanks to the development of the *Robosurge* series of surgical robots, the world's finest surgeons achieve superstar status, performing intricate operations from wherever they are in the world, using satellite links.

2093

110-year-old Daisy Rothenburger wins the much coveted *Golden Scalpel* award for best brain operation, at the fifth Elastoplast International Surgical Awards in Cincinnati. From her remote home deep in the Catskill Mountains and using the latest *Robosurge 3007*, she carried out a full brain transplant on cosmofreight driver Bill Akuba (hospitalized on Mars), who had been injured in a collision with a *Sony Disneytrekker* full of tourists, just this side of Pluto. He is now training to be an accountant with his new brain.

3001

Dr Hans Gruberstein of the University of Dublin announces at a conference that he's finally perfected a memory chip that, once inserted in the parietal lobe of the brain, could improve the memory a thousand times. Unfortunately, says Dr Gruberstein, he's forgotten where he put it . . .

3016

At last a solution as to what to do with our excess old people. The redundant planet *417C* (renamed *Dunroamin*) on the edge of our secondary galaxy, will be converted specially for the aged. Under a massive bubble, kept at a constant 25°C, thousands of trained staff will maintain villages totalling two million old folk. Euthanasia (voluntary death) will of course be available on demand – as will hot milky drinks.

Chapter 5

FIDDLING THE FUTURE

I read this brilliant book the other day by an American guy, James L. Halperin, called *The Truth Machine*. The story starts in the recent past and leads into the future. It was about this kid (who just happened to be a mega-genius) who got the idea that if you could simply invent a machine that was impossible to lie to, all the premeditated (planned in advance) crime in the world would as good as disappear overnight.

But the truth machine isn't simple to invent and a huge billion-dollar company is set up to pay for the research, promising that whoever writes the software programme for it first, would be able to name their price. Everyone would want one – police departments, courts of law (who'd save millions), governments, schools (help!) – and eventually the general public.

Lying or Not

The trouble with the lie detectors (or polygraphs, as they're really called) that we have today, is that they're *fallible* – in other words, they don't really work. Well, they do – sort of – but not for everyone. The polygraph measures the variations of the blood pressure, pulse rate, and breathing of a suspect who's being asked awkward questions (like 'Why did you buy that awful *Bewitched* single?'). Then the operators make their decisions on the results. These lie detectors have been in use since 1924, but still can't be used in evidence against a suspect because, unfortunately, there are a few amongst us (and I'm certainly *not* one of them) who can tell a bald-faced porkie and not move a single muscle or show any other outward or inward signs that a machine could pick up.

Unfortunately, a lie detector that doesn't work for absolutely everyone is a bit like a car that doesn't always start or a boyfriend or girlfriend that only fancies you occasionally. In other words, no flippin' use at all.

Foolproof

So, to get a truth machine that is absolutely impossible to fool would be much more of a stunning breakthrough than you could ever imagine. Just think, you could use it on your mates, your teachers, politicians, life-insurance salesmen and policemen, as well as suspected criminals. What joy! There would be no more ludicrous articles in the tabloid papers, no more loopy reports of creatures from outer space or tall stories of alien spaceships hovering over our back gardens. No more dodgy car dealers and, with a bit of luck, no more tooth fairies or Father Christmases* – the possibilities are endless. On the downside, kids could never tell their parents that they'd done their homework when they hadn't – but then *parents* could never say that they'd always done *theirs* when they were their kids' age.

Best of all, it could well mean the end to all wars, because all the politicians representing the different countries would be forced to say what they really mean, what they really want and what they really plan to do, instead of hiding behind 'diplomacy' (the art of telling whopping lies without upsetting people).

Truth for All

In *The Truth Machine* everyone eventually wore a lie detector on their wrist, so that if anyone told anyone else the smallest fiblet it would bleep and flash – even over the phone. Blimey!

* You miserable old . . . and a Happy Christmas to you too. Ed

Can it Actually Happen?

According to *The Truth Machine* it *can* and *will* happen – it's just a matter of time. But it would be hideously complicated, mainly because the human brain is always changing and evolving throughout a person's life. Having said that, our chromosomes and the genes they contain are currently in the process of being mapped and, once done, scientists could well be on their way.

Useless Pursuit No. 1

How many times a day do we humans tell some sort of fib – small, big, or medium? I think you'd be surprised. Personally, I never lie.*

Farman's Fantasy Future

(with a little help from James L. Halperin)

2003

Millie 'the Geek' Williams, a 13-year-old schoolgirl from Dagenham, Essex, is discovered to be the third richest person in Britain. For over a year she's been hacking into the main computers of most major banks and building societies, creaming off an almost undetectable percentage of every single transaction and depositing her loot in an unspecified Swiss bank account.

2007

Violent crime becomes the major political issue, with murders reaching 50,000 per annum in the US. A new approach to

* That's a lie. Ed

violence, nicknamed 'Two Hits and You're Out', is proposed: anyone found guilty of a *second* violent crime is executed immediately – without going to jail and *without* collecting £200.* This should save 100,000 lives a year. The price? A mere 14,000 executions.

2009

After two years of 'Two Hits and You're Out', violent crime is now down by 50%. Americans claim that at last they are beginning to feel safe on their own streets. Britain is to debate the concept in the Commons and is expected to follow suit before the year is out.

2013

Using an idea borrowed from the 19th century, convicted criminals are now to be sent, not to Australia, but to work on the various space stations currently under construction.

2016

Shock horror, it's official – terrorist groups have now gone nuclear. Police following a group of suspected IRA terrorists stop a driverless car (see Chapter 3) in the Mall, London. In the boot was an Iraqi-made three-megaton nuclear bomb. It was set to go off on reaching its destination – Buckingham Palace – and was estimated to be capable of killing five million people (and a kennel-full of corgis).

2025

After three years of exhaustive tests, it is now established that the *TruthPlus 400* is at last 100% foolproof (even the President of the United States couldn't fool it . . .). It has been designed

* Weak Monopoly joke. Ed

in such a way that no single person knows the whole formula and it has been programmed to change its structure weekly, which means there can be no loopholes whatsoever. Its first practical use will be in the American Courts of Justice where 100 machines are hired at a rate of $5,000 an hour – each. Public lying, from now on, is a thing of the past.

2033

The first case of space piracy occurs when a gang of Malaysian cyberpirates successfully redirect an unmanned *Volvo Cargocruiser* to their 'desert island' – a decommissioned space station currently in orbit round Jupiter.

2047

Dentist Erico Jenkins is executed for what is thought to be the first major crime involving cryogenics. Bostonian Jenkins broke into the Sweet Dreams Cold Home in nearby Woodstock, Vermont – home to 2,700 frozen human residents – and pulled the plug out. It is thought that one of the 'guests'

had a better claim to a large inheritance that Jenkins would otherwise collect.

2600

It is now known that a huge percentage of all known criminals are on the run somewhere in the galaxy. The World Police said today that once a fugitive has managed to leave the Earth's atmosphere there is no practical way of ever catching them.

Chapter 6

FUN IN THE FAR-FLUNG FUTURE

When I was very little,* all that my grandparents had in their house for entertainment was a piano, and their idea of a good night in would be my gran playing a load of old favourites with all the family gathered round singing – badly. Then Grandad saved the day by buying a radio and we all lounged about listening to classics like *Journey into Space, Dick Barton – Special Agent* and *The Goon Show*. My *dad* then went on to buy a massive walnut radiogram on which he would religiously and repeatedly torture us with the only six records that he ever owned.

* Now that *is* history! Ed.

Telly Time

Later, we were lucky to own the first television in our street and I clearly remember, on Coronation Day in 1953, all the neighbours crowding into our front room to watch a young and surprisingly pretty Princess Elizabeth being made a Queen inside that great big wooden box with the tiny little screen.

Tape Time

Then there was a massive leap in technology when I was bought a huge Grundig tape recorder as a reward for passing the 11-plus (the first and last exam I ever *did* pass), on which I recorded (speaker to mike) most of my friends' early rock and roll records (everything *except* Cliff Richard).*

Old Technology

But all this seems like distant history when you look at what's happened over the last few years. As we sail through the millennium, just about everything's gone digital and we can

* Can we get on with it, please? Ed

receive hundreds of different channels on our televisions through cable and satellite. Vinyl records and magnetic tapes have more or less disappeared into that great waste bin we call history. Computer-generated images mean that practically nothing is impossible in movie making, and the special effects that once gobsmacked the world in movies like *Roger Rabbit* and later, *Jurassic Park*, are, as I write, becoming less special by the minute. In the future, just about every form of entertainment (except maybe singing round the piano) will be downloaded from the average family computer, while the scary concept of all-round *virtual reality* looms ever larger . . .

Nearly Real

Virtual reality started as long ago as the 1960s, when fighter pilots trained in simulators with helmets that displayed tracking systems. These developed into the computer games we know and love, in which the viewer can actually participate in the on-screen action. As you can imagine, the technical side of this almost defeats explanation – so I won't try. Already there are virtual reality goggles, headsets, gloves and even whole bodysuits, featuring helmets with stereoscopic screens for each eye, enabling the wearer to travel through a totally simulated environment. If the wearer wears the full kit, all his* movements affect his relationship to this virtual world, and the gloves allow him to touch and handle the 'solid' objects he's faced with. Unbelievable as this seems, experts believe this is just the beginning.

* Or her! Ed

2007

A completely new Beatles album is released, causing a sensation in the record industry. It was produced by the *Dell Digicomp 500* computer (operated by superstar programmer Daronius Doyle) which sampled every note that the four lads ever recorded, examined the thought processes that Lennon and McCartney used when writing the lyrics, and created ten new tracks that experts claim are just as good as the originals. Substantial lawsuits from Paul McCartney (65) who recently bought back all copyright to the Beatles songs, are expected to follow.

2011

Learning a musical instrument could become a thing of the past. Computer wizards at Columbia University produce a computer capable of transposing the sound of the human voice into any musical instrument you choose. This means that by simply humming into the receptor, anything from a saxophone to a double bass can be heard when played back. Whole orchestras will follow.

2018

Never mind *Gladiators,* that daft old TV series of the last millennium (still running on the Telepast network), preparations are now under way for *Realtime Gladiators*, a brand-new series in which contestants pit their wits against unbelievably lifelike lions, bears, bulls and highly trained, heavily armed gladiators in a virtually real AD 50 Roman arena. Any contestant that survives for more than ten minutes will get the thumbs up and win an all-expenses-paid holiday at Ancient World of Rome, Scunthorpe.

2019

Hoverworld, the first ever gravity-free pleasure park, is being planned on Moon Sector 2 by Disney 2000. Although the various themes and rides show endless possibilities, co-sponsor McDonald's (in charge of all intergalactic catering) are still struggling with the headache of how to keep the chips on the plates.

2021

21st Century Fox release a new blockbuster *Some Like it Even Hotter,* an updated version of the classic film *Some Like it Hot* (1959). It stars, believe it or not, all the old favourites – Marilyn Monroe, Tony Curtis and Jack Lemon (all now deceased). The

film, produced entirely by the *Apple Moviescan Computer* in Hollywood, is the first to replicate real people from existing footage from the past. The ex-stars' descendants are believed to have made a small fortune from the rights to reproduce their 'loved' ones.

2126

Michael Jackson, the 166-year-old American rock star of the last millennium agrees to die today. He is believed to be the first person to have changed colour *twice*. Jackson started his life black, became white by middle age and then, in his twilight years, returned to his roots by becoming black again.

2357

Amongst a fury of lawsuits and demonstrations, Francis Albert Sinatra II is born secretly at the Los Angeles branch of Womb-World. He is the first person from the past to be cloned by grafting a sample of his DNA onto a non-allocated synthetic human egg. The DNA sample was sold for an undisclosed sum by the grandson of the murdered Mafia boss, Guido Steffanovanovich, who was thought to have been left alone for a few minutes with Sinatra's body at his burial back in 1998. If allowed to survive, it is thought that young Frank II will be the richest child in the world, just on the strength of future recording contracts and publicity appearances.

4050

All holiday travel is now deemed unnecessary, thanks to the *Disney Virtual Realipod*, soon to become available to every household (a snip at 350,000WD – World Dollars). Simply tap in the exact longitude and latitude of where you want to be,

and the *Realipod* will provide all sounds, smells and sensations without you having to leave your chair. For 20 years, vast teams of Disney employees have painstakingly recorded every inch of the planet using the amazing *Disney Realicord 131*, a machine capable of simulating every aspect of the environment it's placed in.

Chapter 7

UP, UP AND AWAY!

Unless you believe that alien beings are one day going to come down and kindly lead us to other planets when ours gets overcrowded, we are almost certainly going to have to do it ourselves. This might appear a bit pie-in-the-sky now, but it *will* take place, believe me, and – maybe – in *your* lifetime. To say there are problems is an understatement of a fairly major order, but much of the technology is understood even now – it just hasn't been tried out.

Take life on the moon, for instance.

Mooning About

Most of us have seen the pictures of the moon that were beamed back by the astronauts in the early 1970s. Pretty unimpressive unless you're into big, dusty car parks with little craters every few metres. But it must be said that those brave lads landed on the most boring bit because it was easier. The rest of the moon has alarmingly large chasms and valleys caused by the meteors and asteroids that kept hitting it millions of years ago – and who'd want to land there?

Scientists claim that these craters and valleys could be covered over with miles of glass or plastic sheeting (a bit like industrial-strength cling film) and inside this an atmosphere could be produced that would allow the inhabitants to carry on normal lives.

Also on the moon are caves thousands of times the size of our most massive sports venues. These would be a doddle to colonize once one had got all the other basics sorted out – like flushing lavs, parking, etc!

A Mars a Day

Colonizing Mars would be much more tricky (see Great Understatements of Today) because it's further and colder (–60°C on a *good* day). But it does have water by the bucketful (well, by the small frozen bucketful) so if we could create an atmosphere that would sustain life, there appears to be enough of the six chemical elements (oxygen, hydrogen, carbon, nitrogen, sulphur and phosphorus) that we need to last for ever – well almost.

Here's a fairly simple five-point plan to colonize Mars.

☆ Send exploratory expedition with enough sandwiches to last for at least a year (it takes that long for the earth to be in the right position to come home again).

☆ Start heating the place up with immense solar mirrors and paint the mountains black to hold in the heat (simple enough?). Use masses of those nasty gases (the ones that come from fridges and those naff under-arm sprays) that are supposed to be causing the global warming on Earth, to start a nice new global warming of Mars's very own. This alone would raise the temperature enough for humans to be able to walk around without great big, sweaty spacesuits. Genetically tweaked vegetation brought from Earth would start to thrive in such an atmosphere.

☆ Once all the plants begin to take root, the carbon dioxide should split into carbon and oxygen. Clouds would start to form and the sky would turn from pink to blue – which would be jolly nice. By this time the temperature would be a tad below freezing. Proper farming could now begin.

☆ Huge forests would start to appear and plankton (microscopic animal and planty-type things) would start to reproduce themselves in the lakes and seas. This would make the temperature of Mars rise above freezing point.

☆ Cows, pigs, ducks, chickens, wombats – in fact, anything you might need – could be brought on a kind of interstellar Noah's Ark. Towns of Martian pioneer settlers could now start to flourish.

Easy-peasy!

Patience is a Virtue

Before you actually start building a spaceship in your own backyard and asking your mum for a large packed lunch, take heed. Scientists believe that this process, if possible at all, would take at least 150 years and at most 10,000 years, so be prepared to wait a while!

The Quick Way

'But why go to all that trouble?' say other scientists. Why visit planets, which are basically large lumps of rather inconveniently shaped rock, with no air on them? And why go somewhere where you've got to change absolutely everything when it's perfectly possible and probably easier to build your *own* planet to your own design? Let's face it, the only thing limiting the size of space stations so far, has been the supply of materials necessary to make 'em. When did you last hear of a builder's merchant in space? Now we know that

your average asteroid is chock-full of all the materials we could ever need – and that's a fact! It's just a question of catching one.

Useless Fact No. 1077

A kilometre-wide lump of any one of the thousands of small asteroids that whiz about our solar system could supply Earth's industry with most of the minerals and metals it would need for years.

Technically talking, you could make yourself a nice custom-built 'planetette', that could rotate like the earth (giving us proper nights and days) and, with the addition of soil and water, would have lovely valleys and streams (a bit like Surrey) – all plonked in the middle of space. And don't go thinking they'll have to be built by spacemen on ladders: these stupendous constructions of the future will eventually be assembled by fully-automated, self-replicating machines. Not a hard hat in sight (or a builder's bottom*).

Farman's Fantasy Future

2006

A major building to be constructed on the moon, sponsored by massive food giant Nestlé, is also the first space prison camp. The inmates have been taken off death row and given the chance of being space guinea pigs. Under guidance they will build the first completely unmanned chocolate factory – using solar power.

* Please! Ed

2007

Sotheby's are to auction the three ancient electric rover cars left on the moon by the first visitors back in the last century. The old crocks are apparently still in perfect working order (unlike the chaps that drove them).

2009

Happy Eater Hotels announce that they are to open their first orbiting restaurant and drop-in Skytel. They are hoping to attract tourists travelling to and from the future moon and satellite resorts.

2011

Plans for an eighteen-hole golf course on the moon are called off when it was discovered that they needed more than 20 miles between where the ball is struck and the flag. That's gravity (or lack of it) for you.

2013

The dear old Hubble telescope of 1977 is taken out of service and constructed as a tourist attraction at the Spacerama Park on Moon Sector 5. Rather embarrassingly, the very first customer to use it, a little boy, was able to identify, in perfect detail, a tiny moon-shaped tattoo on the behind of a girl who just happened to be sunbathing on Brighton's famous nudist beach.

2021

Solar wings, which use the reflective power of the sun to accelerate them through the vacuum of space, are now under production at Robot Moon Factory 737. These micro-fine, mirrored lightsails will take over all interplanetary cargo transport within five years. After a year spent building up speed, the sails can reach a speed of 100 kilometres per second, pulling almost limitless cargoes. The outer galaxy comes ever closer.

2025

Two hundred men and women today set off from Earth on the first stage of the colonization of Mars. They take with them the revolutionary *Nike 2000 ActiveBody* spacesuit. Programmed to be soft or hard they contain a micron-fine layer of nanomachinery and nanoelectronics. The material, using the patented *ActiveMuscle*, can be as strong as steel while still feeling as soft as a second skin. If required it can amplify movements to give the wearer ten times their normal strength.

The *Nike 2000* is also astoundingly self-repairable when damaged. The almost weightless transparent helmet pumps the purest of air from a lightweight backpack which recycles the carbon dioxide exhaled.

Most miraculous of all, the suit recycles the wearer's waste products by changing their molecular structure into that of a pleasant-tasting and nutritious food. Yum, yum!

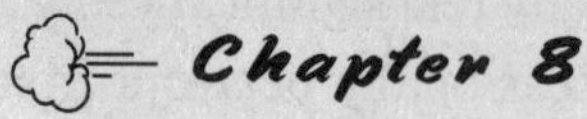

INTO THE WIDE BLUE YONDER

My editor (she's the one who reads the book before it goes to the printer) has told me that I've left a few things out. So here we go, out with the crystal ball for the last time, and let's peer into the future again . . .

Who'll be Running the Show?

As the Third World gradually catches up with the rest of us, it will become increasingly clear that running each individual country separately (be it little or big) is too silly, too expensive, and most of all, too flippin' dangerous! Towards the middle of the 21st century I reckon there'll be a proper World Government with someone like *me* as boss. Alternatively, and more seriously, there could be a small team of 'partner presidents', each picked from a different ethnic group. With a bit of luck this will bring the curtain down on the stupid pantomime called international politics, which we are all forced to put up with now.

Royal Family? Or Not . . . ?

Royalist or not, I'm afraid you are going to have to face the hard fact that our Royal family are approaching a time when they'll be nothing more than a quaint media sideshow* edging towards their sell-by date. Although not disappearing entirely,

* Wait a minute, isn't that what they are now? Ed

they will probably lose any real significance by the early 2020s. King Charles II will occasionally peer out from his home for the 'Ludicrously Rich but Terminally Bewildered', while the

Queen Grandmother (the former Queen Mother – yes, the same one!) – by then totally bionic (having had *all* her body bits replaced) – will still trot out on her birthday to face an audience who will have long forgotten who on earth she actually is.

God or What?

In the not *too* distant future science will be able to explain absolutely *everything* (including the Spice Girls) and therefore there'll be no need for gods. (Before you order a hit squad from the Pope or the Archbishop of Canterbury let me say that that's just *my* opinion.) There will no doubt be an outcry from the major religions, but maybe all those who can't cope with a

religion-free world could be sent off to a spare planet to fight it out among themselves.*

Death is the only thing we can't explain, but by the time most of us are deep-frozen (see Chapter 4), it won't be up to us anyway!

The Last Wedding?

Marriage as an institution will probably end sometime in the next century, to be replaced by a contract linked to the birth of children. When a child reaches 16, parents will be released from any further commitment, but before then both will be held equally responsible.

Baby Boom?

The choice of being able to have a child *outside* the female body (see page 45) will eventually do a lot to equalize the sexes. Children will be rationed on a points system, which will mean that any combination of sexes or groups of people may apply

* I'm glad you said all that and not me. Ed

for a child. Sex, as such, will be for fun only. This could mean that any association of equal members could apply for a licence to have a child, providing they had the right number of points. Points would be awarded according to the results of multi-question tests set by the Child Eligibility Council, a new World Government body. Illegitimacy and unwanted pregnancies would become history.

Whose Class Are You In?

The class system in the future will be related to intelligence rather than breeding or money. Through a variety of taxes, land and loot will be far more evenly distributed. In the distant future, when space colonization is established, every individual will be able to have as much space as he or she wants, which should spell the end of the land-owning classes once and for all.

Edukashun for All?

Sometime in the 21st century, private schools will become a thing of the past. Basically, all learning will be received from interactive computers – ones that will patiently answer all questions . . . and won't get cross when you get things wrong. Teachers will only be there to monitor progress (and make sure the equipment's working OK). Standardized education will mean that a kid from one of our dodgy inner-city areas or even places like Calcutta will have as much chance of receiving a good deal as one from a posh bit of Surrey or Beverly Hills.

Books?

Books (like wot you're reading) will *not* become a thing of the past, as is often predicted, but will become cherished and

valued in the 21st century – not as a learning tool but as a source of unique entertainment.

At school, however, books will relatively soon become a thing of the past – especially where information-gathering is concerned. In the future no one will have to struggle with text that is too difficult (or too easy). It will be adjusted according to the reader's level. At the press of a button on your computer, you will be able to scroll up or down the 'difficultness' scale, until what you are trying to get your head around is presented in a way that you are comfortable with. Also, you'll be able to ask the poor machine as many questions as you like, making learning much more fun and completely removing pressure from your classmates or even the teacher! Three cheers!

Punish the Press?

Sometime in the next few years (maybe even in this government's reign), the responsibility for the lying, nosy, harassing and vulgar articles in *some* of our newspapers (no names need be mentioned) will be put squarely on the shoulders of the papers' owners – at long last. Maybe imprisoning one of the great press barons (and throwing away the key) for what's printed in his paper (*Nude MP in romp with Bishop's butler*, etc.) will finally put a stop to that beastly bunch of smart alecs who produce papers that aren't even fit to use as toilet paper.

What to Wear?

Fashion is one of the only things I'm not prepared to guess at. Let's face it, if I had a clue what people would be wearing tomorrow, let alone in the near and distant futures, I wouldn't be fiddling around writing this daft stuff.*

Any more Sweets?

Twenty-first-century sweets and candy bars will be manufactured so that they are actually *good* for you and will be able to supply you with all the energy you need either for a full day, or at least between meals. Mars Bars, by the way, will eventually be made on the planet they were named after, as a somewhat obvious publicity gimmick.

Sport in Space?

Interest in the big sports like football and cricket will fall as the companies that promote and own the teams become greedier and greedier (making the costs to the fans completely out of reach). In the far distant future a whole bunch of new sports will emerge, based on the various gravitational pulls of the planets. Alternatively, we might be using massive sports centres floating around in the galaxy. Imagine a version of football, for instance, where the players aren't limited to running around on the ground. Just think, goals at the top and bottom as well as at

* And so say all of us. Ed

the sides? Space-sailing could also be popular. Instead of the 'Round the World Race', there could be the 'Round the Moon and Back Race', using zippy solar yachts with large reflective sails that pull in energy from the sun.

Home Help?

Have you ever heard that story of the little old shoemaker who, every morning, when he came down to breakfast, found, to his delight, lots of shoes that had been mysteriously made during the night. Well, in the future, while *we* are asleep, a vast array of pre-programmed household cleaning and maintenance equipment will scurry noiselessly around the house tidying up after us. Interactive robots will wake us up in time for work and school, prepare our breakfasts, and order the self-drive car to be round the front ready for us to leave. I can't wait.*

Foreign Tongues?

One day the world and its satellite planets will all have to have a common language – and it will almost certainly be a form of English (much to the disgust of the French). English is the

* I wish they'd write your books for you! Ed.

language of America and technology – and most of the Internet. Hopefully, however, we will all keep a second language to use where we live. (Actually, this is pretty much the case now.)

To Work or Not to Work

They've said it before, and they'll say it again, in the future most people will be required to work shorter and shorter hours. But this doesn't mean you can throw your school books away and not go to school! It will probably mean that people stop working much earlier (18, I hear you cry) but then they'll have to think of something *else* to do (suggestions on a postcard).

A Future on Earth?

Despite all the fuss about us all dying of cancer from holes in the ozone layer due to the chemicals from fridges, spray cans, fire extinguishers, industrial waste and cows farting, Adrian Berry, in *his* book *500 Years from Now*, claims it's all nonsense. He thinks that if the ozone layer is thinning at all, it's only thinning over the Antarctic because that's the coldest place on Earth and the only place these gases *can* gather. Since hardly anyone lives there, he claims, and since the ones that do live there wear big clothes, it's hardly worth bothering about. As for the 'greenhouse' effect brought on by global warming, he is even more dismissive, claiming that there is no evidence whatsoever to say that it is not due to the natural ebb and flow of the sun's radiation. I don't know about you, but I'm still not going to risk going out in the sun without my factor 30!

Anyway, ozone holes, greenhouse effect or not, it will all be all right in the end, for we'll all be off to other planets fairly

soon – won't we? I for one will be fighting for a place on the first rocket ship off this planet!

What Pets?

Most important of all, who will be our companions on that not-too-distant rocket ship? In the future, with the use of genetic engineering, we will be able to have practically any pet we want. How's about an elephant the size of a dog? Or a whale in a goldfish bowl? But why stop there? Why not have a flying pig? Or a mouse that we can ride? Or an underwater rabbit? Or a four-legged ostrich? Or a lion with a trunk? Or a giant sparrow? Or a singing snake? Or a cuddly shark? Or a furry hedgehog? Or a stripy polar bear? Or a climbing cod? Or a fast-running sloth? Or a fierce worm? Or a barking canary? Or an underwater horse? Or a leaping tortoise? Or a howling goldfish? Or a weeny rhinoceros? Or a one-legged centipede? Or a long-sighted mole? Or a bald sheep? Or a long-haired . . .*

* Yes, Mr Farman, I think we get the point. Ed

TIME'S UP

As you've probably worked out, most of this book was simply guesswork on my behalf – with more than a little help from those clever people who've made a career out of predicting the future. Whatever will happen, however, will happen – and there's not a lot I (or you, for that matter) can do about it.

Depressing? Maybe – but I think it's worth mentioning that despite all the dreadful things that are going on as you read this, the world is a much better place than it used to be – and getting even better all the time. If you don't believe me, try reading some of the other books in this series (£1.99 in all good bookshops). Then you'll see what a really dreadful place the world has been in the past.

The most important thing is that we should all be nicer to each other, and that even includes my editor. Happy reading!